Unforgetting

Unforgetting

Poems by

Christine Potter

Kelsay Books

Cover: "Piermont Home" by Nancy Quaglia, oil on canvas

ISBN: 978-1-947465-97-8

Kelsay Books
Aldrich Press
www.kelsaybooks.com

For my husband Ken, and for my family—especially my mother Gloria and my sister Susan.

And in loving memory of our Desmond Jones (aka Desmond T. Cat, esq.), a giant among kitties.

Acknowledgements

Some of these poems first appeared in:

Autumn Sky Poetry, The Literary Bohemian, Rattle, Eclectica, The Eclectica 20th Anniversary Anthology, The Pedestal, The Peacock Journal, Beauty First: The Peacock Journal Anthology, Fugue, Ithaca Lit, American Arts Quarterly, The Anglican Theological Review, The Scarborough Presbyterian Church Newsletter, The Axe Factory, The Crab Orchard Review, and *The Raintown Review.*

Thanks especially to Christine Klocek-Lim at *Autumn Sky Poetry,* Tim Green at *Rattle,* and Jen Finstrom at *Eclectica.*

"The House We Didn't Buy" was nominated for a Pushcart Prize by *Eclectica* "After The Ghost Investigation" was also nominated for a Pushcart, by *Autumn Sky Poetry.*

"Hibakusha" was an IBPC winner in May, 2015.

"This Dangerous Agreement" was written for ABC Radio News' *America Celebrates,* and broadcast by them on July 4, 2017. Thanks to Aaron Katersky and Treavor Hastings.

Many of these poems were first drafted during writing marathons at The Waters online poetry workshop. Thanks to Toni Clark, Jude Goodwin, and to all who participate there!

The cover painting, as always, is by my dear and generous friend Nancy Quaglia.

Contents

Lunch on City Island, Early June

We sat outside. Noon leaked through rain a long way off,
grew quiet and then quieter as light can, even falling
on vinyl palm trees wired with light-up coconuts. Silver,

white, a splash of brown—the Sound was the color of gulls
circling it, and rippled with coming weather. Still wearing
a graduation gown that puffed around her like a black sail,

a tall young woman carried a plate piled with fried fish
to a table beside us. You bought me a too-full plastic glass
of white wine pale as tap water, which turned out to be

delicious, or at least made me notice how richly green
the trees were, how ancient and tangled with each other and
rooted here as long as my family. I drank and was content,

although not an hour ago, my mother had refused to see
her doctor, had narrowed her eyes at me and spat out
her pills, but looked cheerful if confused when we finally

left her house. So I told you about my friend Zack, who
opened the roof of his convertible on a huge blue day to
drive to his class reunion, when the brilliance or perhaps

weight of the sky overwhelmed him and he was frightened.
It was funny in the telling, but now I know the truth of such
burdens, their unexpected heft. Of course, he kept driving.

What choice is there? A quick gust snatched my napkin,
which floated past my hands into the Sound and dissolved.
Calamari and fried shrimp, clouds dull as chain-link fences.

So many apartment windows across the water, so many cars
lined up on the roads and bridges. Red and green lights.
The hush of doctors'offices. And rain coming, coming rain.

Save the Human Race

Although she never did before, my mother lies.
She doesn't have dementia. She answers questions

like someone drinking white wine at a dinner party,
pretending to have read the best-seller: *of course*

I went to church! There was a skirt, she says, *and
a dress—the same pattern? Red. I wore one of those.*

The one we tried on Friday? I ask. A silence.
She takes a breath, relieved: *Yes!* The secret she

doesn't have is safe. My father has been counseled
not to argue with her, or has his hearing aid off.

I think he's going to say North Korea is planning
to nuke Hawaii, where my sister is on vacation, but

he's into economic inequality and arthritis instead.
At least I don't have to explain why I believe this is not

the worst time civilization has ever known, remind
him to take his pain-killers, cite The Civil War or

The Black Death. He's in a good mood. He tells me
about the diversionary mission he never flew with

his Air Force unit, the medical discharge just in time.
I feign surprise; he's shared this secret with my sister,

not me. *So now we both know,* I type into the email.
Dad wouldn't have been one of the few survivors.

I think about not being anything at all, a missed beat,
a bright white screen with nothing on it. I hit send.

Outside, little brown and grey birds peck at the feeder.
A young hawk, mumbling his hunger, misses them

and takes off. And a jet in the cloudless sky is a silver
brooch on a white ribbon, up so high I can't even hear it.

Watching My Mother's Heart Beat

At midday, the exam room's dark as day care nap time:
five-year-olds on blue fold-out mats, the bright line
of sun beneath a drawn shade. My first teaching job.

A boy's tiny leg marks air-circles as he lies on his back,
half-dreaming, gazing up to watch the clock of his foot—
until I hear the technician's fingers click computer keys

and stop remembering him. Onscreen, the green fist
of my mother's heart tightens and relaxes. Becomes
two dancers swishing in and out to the beat of our

old washing machine. The technician rings the scene
in light the way I once wrote my name with a sparkler.
My mother smiles. She says nothing. She remembers

different things on different days. Perhaps it's all truth:
her silence, the light the technician and I record in our
different ways, this electronic tide, the path of its flow.

What I still can't see is if my mother was ever happier
than she was angry. Even now. Even now, I don't know.

Showing My Father My iPhone

My father says what's wrong with digital photography
is that no one ever prints anything out and so this
flood tide of imagery clogging the internet will

be lost, *lost* in fifty years, along with fair politics, the
environment, the economy, and all passion for history's
grim lessons. *You never print anything out*, he says

and shows me a Photoshopped portrait of my mother
in her thirties walking the ocean's edge, sandals
dangling from her left hand's loose fingers: but on

paper! Saved! He has ratcheted up the focus and
color so much that the image is beaded, pointillist,
a clunky mosaic. *I couldn't do that in the darkroom*,

he says. *This is how to use the technology!* It's hard
to tell from the picture how beautiful my mother was
in 1950: the triangular scarf tied over her hair, her

movie-star waist, her steps in the sand graceful as ivy.
You used to take decent pictures, he says, *but you don't
even use a camera anymore, just this damn phone.*

You could do professional quality stuff if you tried.
I taught you. I take a breath and tell the truth: my
Zeiss Ikon Contessa and exposure meter lugged

all through high school only to please him, my adult
understanding that I never will. He laughs the squeaky
giggle that means he's won: *You still take pictures;*

you put them on Facebook. Print them out instead!
I don't want to do professional quality stuff, I say, but
he's back onto election fraud and immigration policy.

My mother has lost track of the conversation again.
She leans forward to stare at nothing, and is still lovely.
I take the phone from my father to snap her picture.

Dressing My Mother

She wouldn't let me do it at first. Now
she comes upstairs with me, wordless

as I find the Mother's Day blouse from
two years ago, tags still attached, stuffed

in the back of her closet, the blue jeans
my sister probably bought her, or maybe

I did. I can't remember, either. I forget
when she started forgetting. Her room

overflows with gifts she won't wear unless
I hold the arms out for her, match a scarf,

fluff her hair. The store where I bought her
silver dragonfly pin has been closed for

how long? Once, she reminded me I didn't
know so much; she'd paid for both of my

weddings, for all the good it did her. That's
long gone now, too: cologne evaporated

in a pressed glass bottle, lost amid her
dresser's clutter, too pretty to throw away.

Escape Mechanism

After a year of driving the fancy car that was my mother's before
she began to forget, I finally clean its trunk: lose outdated maps

I'd first thought I might need, fold and stow the sticky blue tarp
for its annual turn hauling Christmas trees, find a paper fan that

opens into a pleated circle of cherry blossoms and vanishes back
into itself. Put that in the glove box. Toss a tragic hair brush

missing half its bristles and the empty, wide-mouthed bottle I fear
my father kept close at hand on longer trips. Have I said this car

is too good for me, too graceful, too powerful, with seats that heat
at a button-push and a tinted window overhead sliding open to

let in the sound of dry leaves scratching across back roads, the last
few crickets, the blurred bass thump of a party a block distant?

I turn off the ignition believing I really do deserve to purchase
ruinously-priced jars of Italian artichoke cream at the market

where worried young mothers frown at food labels. But I have
no children, my own mother is too old for such concerns, and now

I drive her car. Shall I should say what else I found in its trunk?
The leather-bound owner's manual calls it *The Phosphorescent*

Handle: yellow-green, plastic, with a wordless black arrow. For
escape in certain emergencies. Please note the handle will glow

longer if exposed to bright light. My mother never told me this last secret: *you, too, can be stolen, just like anything else. Fortunately*

a plan is in place. Someone else did the worrying, so you needn't fret. Ease your foot onto the accelerator. It is now safe to forget.

Unforgetting

I think of my mother when I write fiction,
how she lost the way Chopin and Bach laid
their hands over hers while she practiced piano
like the kind uncles they weren't, how she lost

New York City's silky grey sky outside
her desk's 16th floor window at Macmillan,
lost even her squat, stop-sign-red Correcting
Selectric typewriter. I think of how she

remembers what she cannot remember.
The stories flood away from her but still
she scoops them to her lips and tells them.
This shouty new hamburger joint must

be the place where she went dancing after
the War. And didn't I love Spotty the terrier,
who nipped at the grocer's delivery boy
twenty years before I was born? I can't

say no. There's a Juliet Balcony in Verona, a
Headless Horseman Bridge in Sleepy Hollow.
And at Winchester Cathedral, a dazzling
maze of stained glass smashed to bits by

Cromwell, but leaded back together in
the Restoration—kings' heads, the hands
of saints, all out of context and bright as
anything broken, beautiful and gathering light.

After Easter Vacation

the school year, which had been endless, begins to careen
down the hot, shiny steel of a tall slide in the Elementary
playground. So many saddle-shoe steps to climb its ladder!
Boys behind you tug the bow-tied belt of your dress: *Cooties!*

Slowpoke! And then you're at the bottom. Coarse sand
meant for cushioning falls fills your socks, and then there's
the back and forth squeak of someone pumping too high
on the worn canvas seats of the swings. Your teacher holds

a red grade book against her chest as she stands in the shade
talking to another teacher who looks exactly like her, the blue
arms of both their sweaters looped around their necks, a breeze
coming off the River. Years later, you become a teacher yourself

and lift your classroom window to that same breeze. Your
desk chair wears your suit jacket. It's National Poetry Month.
Your students are bored, although they do find it amusing
you're a poet. They tell you the sonnet you wrote for them

is dumb, but ask you to read it again, just to waste time. That's
when you suddenly remember the word "seersucker," how you
had a shirtwaist made of it the spring you were seven. It was
knee-length, green and white—at first only for church, but

the next year a school dress that stayed loose and cool even
when you ran all the way home from the bus stop, pursued
by those same boys. How puckery and light it felt under your
fingers! You clear your throat and read the sonnet again.

What I Intended

I never intended to have this life, believe me—It just happened
—Robert Bly

My mother was full of advice and I was
dumb enough to ask for some. My head
shoved deep into the kitchen sink until
my neck hurt, my hair full of Breck suds,

my eyes squinted shut so hard behind
the damp, folded-over towel that it was
like holding my breath, I still asked,
but knew her answers: *They tease you*

because they like you. Ignore them and
they'll stop. Really, Christine, you bring
these things on yourself. That wasn't true,
except she was an adult and had to be right.

I knew how much they hated me. *Don't*
use that word, she said. *Children can't*
understand what it means. She rinsed
my hair. *No one hates you,* she said. But

they lived next door to us, ran me up the
hill from the bus with bits of Mr. Gowen's
gravel driveway in their pockets, to throw.
Ugly! Ugly! Ugly! they chanted, even

though when my hair dried, it gleamed
like the back cover of *Family Circle.* They
didn't hate my sister, who was smart
enough to keep her mouth shut. What I

intended was to grow all the way up into
the clouds, my blonde hair shining like
an incoming tide on Cape Cod, where I
was often happy. Instead, we all fell away

from each other. Instead we all pretended
to like each other. Instead, everyone's
father died and we forgot everything but
the green smell of crushed dandelion stems.

Instead, I have this quiet house in which I
write these true words, a freight chuffing
towards the mile-off crossing, the black
and white train of what I intended to say.

Power Failures

were why as a child I loved great storms,
gales that might loft fifty years' worth

of maple tree through a bedroom window—
and then the hurricane's nightmare-still Eye.

Could it really see us? *Look at that fool Pugh,*
my mother said. Outside our sun porch windows,

there he was, shirtless in the sodden air,
tossing broken branches into a pile in his yard.

That wind could start up again any minute,
she said, and I waited for him to be struck dead.

He wasn't. He was wearing his old army pants.
He was a Marine in The War, I said. She got up,

rolling her eyes. The outside light was green.
Inside, everything looked like fairytales, gold as

the kerosene in our old glass lamps. Held to their
flame, even my tumbler of ginger ale glowed. *Don't*

do that, my mother said, and thumped upstairs. I
stocking-foot skated into the kitchen, opened our

back door. *You stay inside*, she called, *I mean it!*
The neighbor's willow hung limp as long, wet hair.

The puddle I stepped out into was warm: magic!
I wished the power would never come back on.

Kickball

Like everything else, it was mostly about waiting,
especially for me, lost in the furthest-out exurb
of the kicking order, then sent to the outfield: *Way,*

way out in the outfield, as Sandy would say. She
dropped either my sister or me off the top bar of
our swing set, telling us it was the same thing

as a circus tight rope—except perfectly safe. Sandy
was Captain of the Team always, her scowling face
sidewalk-tough as she ran to meet the bowled ball

and launch it toward Ashford Avenue. How odd
that I don't remember which of us fell—Susan or
me—or anything about how that must have felt:

letting go of Sandy's hand, one queasy step, the
futile grab at a swing's aluminum chain, and then
the cruel truth of the ground, the all-over ache of

having lived. Sandy was a year older than me. She
had the only male teacher in our elementary school.
He'd sewn her costume for the school play: green

and purple silk, leg o'mutton sleeves. He'd made
her Queen of Something. I stood below her parents'
picture window and marveled at what I'd seen in

the twilit auditorium just a few hours before: same
girl, same dress. I knew then her life would never
be mine. Mostly, I'd be waiting for my up, the ball

skittering toward me across tar and asphalt. Mostly I'd be pulling back my right foot to kick it and not *(Oh, God!)* stumble. And mostly, I'd be out at first.

On Holy Saturday

for Ahmie, my great-aunt

By the time my great-aunt showed up with
Little Golden Books fresh from the supermarket
for my sister and me, my parents' fight was over

but my father was still down in the basement
running his table saw and shouting *Oh, SHIT*
between its violent complaints. *Don't ever*

say that, said Ahmie to me. *Bad men in prison
say that.* And she gave us the books, which opened
stiffly because they were so new. *Oh, God, not*

again, my mother said. *They'll never learn
to read if you keep buying them that garbage!*
My father said *FUCK!* and turned on a drill.

My aunt was sad then, and not because she was
a widow. *There's a pall hanging over this house,*
she said and all at once I was frightened and sure

she meant Poll Parrot, who sold children's shoes
on TV but was worse than any monster because of his
terrible, nasal voice. I wondered where Poll was and

suddenly understood how he could be invisible.
Jesus Christ was already dead but yet unrisen.
A black-clad priest on educational TV finished his

show about the Shroud of Turin: mummy wrappings!
I'd eat myself sick on candy the next day. Now I was
just waiting. There was a pall, a shroud, a nasty

silence worse than curses. But the sun wouldn't
stop and the neighbor's cherry tree was a pink
waterfall, weeping and weeping and weeping.

What My Sister Made

Yet another Abstract-Expressionist swirl of crayon, a
whole box of them clutched in her fist, a nest of colors
that read mostly brown. On the wall, hidden behind
a door we didn't close. So when Mom finally found it,

she couldn't know the date of its making. No small,
waxy spasm, either; this was tall as Susan stood at four,
a true mural, a scribble carved finger-cramp deep into
the wallpaper. *She doesn't know better*, Mom said, but

I was three years older, and nasty as a knotted shoelace.
It looks awful! I sang. Susan cried, and I was Spoken To.
She didn't get in trouble for making a fat snowman of
mashed potatoes, carrots, and peas, for leaving its

dotty green smile on top of the stove. Or slipping eggs,
ketchup, and breadcrumbs out of the kitchen, trying to
turn the living room couch into a meatloaf. I waited
until that she was elbow-deep in that to tell, but knew

nothing would happen. Susan's tears were silvery
as the tinsel she hung on the Christmas tree, strand
by strand, instead of dashing it on in handfuls, like me.
Meatloaf! said Mom at supper. And my father smiled.

Zion Episcopal Church, 1962

I was in choir already, my purple, overcoat-heavy robe
weighting me nearly into sleep. The scent of brass polish,
the scent of lemon oil, Father Carsten's white hair like
baby bird fluff on his nearly-bald head, bronze-lit

by stained glass near the many-times-varnished
pulpit. I thought of his wife's fur stole: little foxes
with their heads still on, each biting the other's tail to
hold it around her neck. Maybe I wanted one exactly

like that. How pleasant to be bored, pleasant to be
too warm, fading in and out of the snore of so many
words. It might even take until Christmas to get to
Communion. But suppose it only took until summer?

We'd be in Cape Cod then, where we never went to
church. I looked at Jesus with His lap full of children
in the window over the high altar. His hair was golden
brown, like my mother's and sister's. In waves. Waves

on the beach at Cape Cod, biting each other's tails, like
Mrs. Carsten's stole. *In Joseph's lovely garden, the Lord
Christ's tomb was made.* Easter scared me more than
Halloween, all those lilies growing out of what? Michael

the acolyte passed out last year, but only long enough
to brag about it later. Father Carsten didn't even notice.
The service went on. The service always went on. Bells,
the hoot of the organ, that endless, Zen, Episcopalian hum.

Singing My First Funeral

I think his last name was Messerich. His first...Charlie?
I think so. I hear my father's voice saying it with

that friendly lilt men use to mean a good guy: Charlie
Messerich, church sexton during those few years Dad

tried believing what the rest of us did. Charlie's funeral.
Everyone else was still alive. Sextons cleaned, fixed things—

but clearly not everything. Like having to die. Zion Church
looked embalmed as ever: dim, airless, polished, Victorian—

even with Sputnik twinkling in circles over our heads.
Someone else must have cleaned, I thought, and wondered

why I couldn't cry. I knew you were supposed to. One girl
whose name I've also lost crayoned a picture: a man labeled

Charlie Messerich leading the Junior Choir skywards, all
our arms out straight before us like movie monsters, all

our kimono-sleeved choir robes dragging behind us on
pink and orange clouds. Melissa, maybe. I'd watched her

roll Italian bread into little balls and swallow handfuls
of them at the Spaghetti Dinner. Kids said her parents had

to call the ambulance and get her stomach pumped. Would
she have died? She cried at the funeral, and I could not.

Hymns. An anthem. It was just more church, and not
even Good Friday. I never asked her about her stomach.

Afterwards, I took off my starchy collar and freed my hair
and bobby pins from my choir beanie for The Reception

in The Parish Hall. Everyone's mother smiled through
a haze of heated-over ham and pineapple slices too dense

for me to want any. I don't think I ever cried, even later,
back home. I scuffed the soles of my patent leather shoes

all the way to my parents' car. All afternoon, everything
was too bright, like staring at a bare light bulb. Like Heaven.

My Grandfather, At Work Building Indian Point Nuclear Power Plant

There's an old picture of him—reds gone orange—
on a tractor, containment dome half-built
behind his flannel-shirt shoulders. I remember

the huge hole, the stones saved for my rock collection,
passed to me from the rough hands of his coworkers:
granite, mica to flake with a finger, smoky quartz.

Fifth grade. An assembly in the auditorium, the scent
of floor wax and scorched celluloid. The Friendly Atom
on the movie screen, electrons zipping in circles like

The Steeplechase ride at Playland. A deep-voiced
announcer calm and wise as Moses said exactly when
The World's Nations were about to run out of oil,

this invisible miracle would spark up and save
the day. *How kind of God to plan so well!* I thought.
The Cyclotron was right up Route 9 at Columbia Labs.

I'd seen it. And my very own grandfather was building
Indian Point so I could watch Dick Van Dyke on TV.
Even the Hudson River was conveniently placed: I knew

they needed water for The Plant. So why, after school,
did I walk behind the train station all alone and gather
ugly stones sticky with tar? They were nameless,

of course, and hot from sitting in the afternoon sun.
I threw each one into the river as hard as I could
until my hands were empty, until my right arm ached.

My Irish Grandmother, Noreen

Not the German one, plump and black-haired at
sixty-two, she whose white-gold chicken gravy—
unbothered by herbs or pepper—was like pouring
sunlight on snow. Not Nana Ethel. Nana Noreen,

whose kitchen was dark as a closet, a creaky Otis
elevator ride up an apartment building in the
part of Yonkers my father couldn't wait to leave.
Always, it was Sunday night there. Always her

windows were locked—drafty mirrors turning
everyone translucent. Cold cuts for supper and
potato salad with bacon. A bedroom that was
once her dead sister's, its hard, high bed and the

faint, cedar-y smell of mothballs. Riding home
in the car, Mom said, *Your father insists I make
a double recipe of icing, because his mother
was so stingy with the sugar.* But Nana's cake

was fine. How much sugar did you need? I
couldn't tell them I liked her religion, too, the
saints' cards, the candles, the whole of Heaven
and Hell set up like a corporation, with glass

doors and secretaries, maybe. Like the places
my parents worked. So why couldn't they see?
Mortal sin was only a Disney witch's spell. You
got saints' days off school instead of cotton puffs

to glue on brown construction paper in the damp
Episcopal basement. (And why was it always about
sheep?) Nana Noreen's hug was too tight, bony
as a broken chair. The sugar wasn't an issue at all.

Wallpaper

My German grandmother's house had rooms with names.
The Sun Porch was inside, not out—and had, over its musty
bamboo couch, a picture of dawn-lit goddesses reclining

beside Greek columns and silver pools. The Liberty Room
was more confusing: a bedroom where no one slept. With
a maple vanity where you were supposed to sit and apply

lipstick, gazing into a three-sided mirror. But I was only
old enough to brush my hair. Instead of shirts and dresses,
the closet was full of a staircase where my grandfather

had once killed a whole hive of wasps. Did Liberty mean
an attic escape into darkness and empty trunks? Afraid
to ask and be laughed at, I finally read the wallpaper.

In faded pink and ivory, groups of Colonial gentlemen
signed The Declaration of Independence over and over—
in each corner and around all the windows. Smiling ladies

in ball gowns just waved fans. And above them rose
Independence Hall in Philadelphia, its pink stories piled
one on the next like the many layers of my mother's

wedding cake. In her white lace dress, she'd been beautiful
as the wallpaper women, and my sister looked like her.
Everyone said I looked like my father, but I was supposed

to be a girl. It didn't make sense unless things eventually
turned into whatever you called them, the way women's
last names became their husbands'. Simple as wallpaper.

The House We Didn't Buy

dangled over Broadway, probably with Hudson
River views from its top story. I couldn't force
myself to climb that far. It was dark, derelict,

walls the long-absent color of dust and shadows.
Concrete sealed the toilet bowl. There was wind.
Autumn sunshine flickered beneath the battened

bathroom windows, cold and golden on all that
ugliness. I was eleven and sure the house had been
murdered and left unburied. I was old enough not

to be so silly. Even my little sister went upstairs.
But I had to run outside shaking, and stare from
the dizzy brink of the front yard down four long,

rickety flights to our family's nearly-as-ruined
white convertible. My parents chased bargains.
They said they'd fix up the house, but then we'd

have to live there. Except we never did, and not
because I cried. I didn't. I was too sad to cry,
so for once I kept quiet and dreaded a future

that didn't happen. Years later, someone else
sided the place, killing what I now recognize
as gracious Edwardian lines. Still, I can't imagine

anyone happy there. That house held its anger
tight as the inside of a fist. We would only have
painted it over. It would have swallowed us.

Your Favorite Beatle

You had to have one. (That and a Troll Doll:
plastic, half a foot high, flame of frizzy hair
erupting from its grinning head. Nude, sold
that way, but some girls in your class sewed

clothes to fit them, which made yours seem
even more naked.) Anyway, you chose John.
Your sister beat you to Paul, the prettiest.
You couldn't like the same one. Also, you had

to wear fishnet stockings. They garroted
the soft flesh of your legs when you knelt
in church, trying not to think of Paul or John,
even when their names came up in Scripture.

Your sister was younger. She embraced
such things with joy. You had to pretend to
be disgusted at her conformity. What relief
when John proved himself to be the smart one

and you found in your grandmother's house
a round pair of gold-rimmed glasses that could
have been wonderful on you if your eyes hadn't
been young and keen. (You never really hated

Yoko.) Years later, when you finally needed
readers, you remembered your reflection: black
turtleneck, bell bottoms, the mirrored world
blurred by your great-grandfather's prescription.

You had looked just like John: not the same
as screaming for him (you'd never have done it)
or going out with him (it would have been
awkward). But for that moment, it was enough.

Personal Typing at Dobbs Ferry Junior High School

My guidance counselor, who had a TV
fortune teller's five o'clock shadow on her
upper lip at 9:23 AM, said I had to take it
although I was supposed to be Academic, not

Business Tracked. For college English papers,
assuming I got in. She said I might not marry
and clearly had no head for math except
one space after commas, two after periods.

So, thirty royal blue Selectrics that clacked
to "The Syncopated Clock" on a crackling LP,
and Mr. Petronis, his aftershave and sharply
tailored jacket smiling at me when I hit sixty

words per minute clean: *How does it feel
to be Top Typist in Personal?* The bell rang
and he held me back. I should consider
Business Track. I could have a real future.

I wouldn't need more science. He was old
as a glass jar of formaldehyde frogs, old as
our history books that petered out after
World War II. And he knew my parents.

I couldn't tell them what he'd said because
they'd believe him. My only talent: typing.
It turned my stomach like sour milk. Still,
I space twice after periods the way he taught,

although it's archaic. My thumb can't stop
making room for something that was once
important—but not breath, or love, or God.
Maybe just an office door, left blessedly open.

Walking Home Alone

Was I hearing "Downtown" or "Slow Ferry
'Cross The Mersey?" A red transistor radio,
the scent of moss and mud. All done with
junior high. I'd been afraid to love those

songs, except by myself, far from the JV
cheerleaders who chanted them nasally
on our lurching school bus, far even from my
own sister, who happily bought hit singles

to play over and over until I couldn't walk
without their lyrics blown into every breath,
every step past the rusted gates and broken
driveway of a mansion that wasn't even

there anymore. A tangle of wild raspberries,
a sweaty hill, and ahead of me a British boy
from my class with a withered arm. Some pill
his mother took, everyone said. He was sweet

if you talked to him, but wasn't The Beatles,
so he walked alone, too. He lived nearby in
the big house that was still there. I leaned into
my radio and wondered what music he liked.

His name was Steve. He wasn't with me
but I wished he was. My too-new, pointy
white sneakers. My family about to move.
And the lawns and trees so green, so green.

In 1972: Five Poems

1. College Radio

The studios with their nursery-school blue walls
always smelled of sawdust and ancient paper—
newly built but somehow older than our parents,

many of whom had already reclaimed our bedrooms
for dens back downstate. We had no faculty advisor.
We taught one another to spin the record backwards

three-quarters of a turn from the beginning of the track
and keep the microphone turned off in case someone
said *shit!* Evan believed the FCC listened in Buffalo

with special receivers to pick up our 10 watts, and
therefore we shouldn't play songs that glorified drugs.
One Toke Over The Line was the most obvious, he said,

and clogged its grooves with purple crayon. The AM
Top 40 place up the hill pumped it out twice an hour.
That winter, I'd tried to stop seeing a poet named Pete,

who drooled over my poems in Workshop thrice weekly.
He lived upstairs from the station. He set his dirty
underwear on fire trying to purify it with incense. We

watched charred cotton scraps of it float down and
land in the snow outside the control room: hiss, hiss.
During the mining of Haiphong Harbor, we sat up late,

cross-legged on the floor in the newsroom, yellow reams
of UPI stories spooling out over our heads. We talked
about the Book of Revelation. Weren't there nukes at

the Seneca Army Depot? No escape, not even home in
Westchester! Someone said a history prof was running
away to Fiji with a student nanny. Could that be true?

When the world didn't end, we propped text books
up against the mixing board and studied for finals
on the air. I moved out of my dorm room to stay

with a friend so I could do my last show, the week
school closed. Her dad was German. *There she goes—
Rah-dio Free Europe*, he said, as I dragged grey

wooden crates full of LPs over dandelions on his
lawn, loading somebody's southbound car. Locusts
moaned a cue tone for an upcoming program about

which I hadn't been informed. The trees' green was
like fire, the air so hot it vibrated. Pete kept calling
my parents' house. My mom took all his messages.

2. College Rock Critic, Female

You couldn't tack up the wrong poster
over your bed. The album's second side
had to be perfect as slouching on a creaky

front porch the first almost-warm day,
holding a finger-aching-cold bottle of beer.
The hit songs you didn't sneer at needed

45

something hard-to-notice: percussion that
was really hand claps in a cement-walled
stairwell, one of the Beatles playing solo

under a made-up name. And if the singer-
songwriter was also a woman, you'd need to
apologize for her voice unless she sang in

a deeper range than most men, even if
the production made up for it and wasn't
her guitar work amazing? (Knowing the

name of that last diminished chord was
going overboard; keep it to yourself.) But
you were usually right. The guy you hoped

to impress would smoke a joint with you—
and leave. At least the air outside your dorm
would be sweetly blue then, and you could

put on something sappy and acoustic. But
forty-five years later, he'd come to your house
for Thanksgiving with a thick folder of all

your undergrad columns. You'd be long-
married, he long-divorced: Oz behind the
curtain, revealed. What dear magic it is to

be twenty, world-weary, and correct! What
dear magic it is to not be, your silly old
words left to chase their own nervous truth.

3. Receptionist

The men weren't in charge. My mother was,
at her desk by the tall Third Avenue window:
Executive Secretary. The men tried to get me
drunk at lunch on magnums of cheap white wine

at the Indian restaurant by the River, and kept
taxidermied piranhas on their giant desks. I sat
out front, behind an even larger desk, guarding
a door two guys high, all summer. I was nineteen.

Mom had already taught me to drink Beck's Dark
and whiskey sours. *Fun City!* said the mayor. I
was no easy prey. My acid-addled ex-boyfriend
cried on the couch in the lobby when I told him

to go away, his muddy eyes matching the awful
wall panelling. *He seemed a nice young man,*
someone said. The pay was good. I typed poems
on the Correcting Selectric with its magic white

ribbon that could lift mistakes right off the page.
The phone seldom rang. It was fine to crack jokes
when it did. I thought the job easy. Once, I watched
a solar eclipse with Mom, from her desk, and the

midtown air went grey as someone dying. *There's
a blackness in everything,* Mom said, *even light.*
The real receptionist returned from vacation, and I
went back to school. As always, my mother was right.

4. Hanging Out on the Old Croton Aqueduct

Dobbs Ferry, NY

The last thing we thought of was water but
the old pipes to The City were still there,
beneath a grassy trail that led only to more

of itself. It was Middle Earth, or pen and ink
drawings from a book of fairy tales, with round
stone towers two hands taller than our heads,

like toy castles. Someone had read they were
ventilators left over from 1840 and always
said so as we passed them. Then we all knew,

and forgot about them. We drank beer, or
when we were stupid, Southern Comfort,
which was like swallowing pine cones instead

of kicking them as we walked. Twenty-six
miles from The Bronx to The Dam, in Croton.
No one jogged then, so no adults—except for

one man mowing the shady back yard of his
enormous house in Irvington. He ignored us.
We ducked back behind Mercy College, to the

nuns' cemetery with its Stations of the Cross,
each sad and holy scene set in what looked like
a bird house. I found them beautiful and knew

better than to say so. We never hiked all of it.
The trail could have been a foreign country,
or even endless. Home from college, guitars

dangling upside down over our shoulders,
we ended up at Jimmie's, ordering manicotti,
baked clams, Chianti in a rattan basket. And

my brother wiped everyone's plate clean with
a heel of Italian bread. The chef came out to
pound his shoulder. *You're a good boy!* he said.

5. At the Abandoned Estate

Half a mile of thimbleberry bramble.
A carpet of winter-bleached maple leaves
rotten with snow melt, our steps soft on

granite stairs caked with years of mud. All
the way up the side of a brick basement
missing its manor house. Our legs dangling

over two stories of empty air and shadow
to see the Hudson's blinding flash, its silver
slash behind a scraggle of March trees and

the hiss of distant traffic. Me at nineteen.
I could barely hear wherever it was we'd
left the car, but wasn't afraid of the boy

who'd hiked with me there, was glad to
smoke the joint he bare-finger snuffed after
two hits, was glad to cough and laugh

and upend beer bottles from my backpack
or maybe his, the amber glass glinting,
sweating, almost too cold to hold in

the river's last winter breath. What mercy
kept us from washed-out mortar, loose
stones, sudden tree roots, and the clunk

of his uncertain transmission? What grace
kept us dreaming backwards, beyond
ballrooms burned, past kitchens fallen in

and saw us home safe and chattering
about Prohibition and F. Scott Fitzgerald
while the dying sun gilded all that waste?

Hometown

Sunset light on brick buildings from the
1920's: square, no-nonsense store fronts.
Long-legged teenagers walk like cut-loose
marionettes, heads down, in twos and threes—

clumps of them hunched under backpacks,
spilling into traffic. I am either their age or
my own, but it doesn't matter because today
what I remember is joy. Joy in the silence

before my parents got home from work,
the moment before the needle dropped
onto the LP. Before passing time limited
the size of the world, or the prickly caress

of a cold afternoon, my dry-cleaner stiff
winter coat tossed on a chair in the kitchen.
I still hear the record: Simon and Garfunkel
or Vivaldi and now the sun is down behind

the Palisades. Bare trees framing pink air
like lead and stained glass. I must be some
age or another, in my bedroom, alone at home.
I must be hungry and not even know it.

Poem to Myself at 30

I see you change out of your whites
in the cooks' bathroom where
a florescent tube, almost burnt-out,
flickers like Charlie Chaplin. Garlic

stings your cuticles, a clingy musk
under the lavender hand soap
someone else brought in. Take off
your bandana, shake out your flat hair,

and open the door to the sudden
comfort of the wide black sky
overhead: no moon, but stars and
stars and stars. The bread order

is placed, tomorrow's vegetables
safe in the dill-scented walk-in. Try
not to listen to your mother. It's fine
to be happy with this. See? Your

old red car still runs smoothly.
It radio is tuned to a friendly song,
and the drive uphill and home
shorter and kinder than you think.

The Wildlife of Seattle and Whidbey
Island, Washington

Instead of packing for the flight to Seattle or walking
on the treadmill, I talk to my mother about polar bears.

She's sure she has seen polar bears in Seattle, on a stroll
with my father through my sister's neighborhood. She

cautions me to play dead if I see one, so it won't eat me.
I think of the movie about climate change, the tragic white

bear who climbed, hungry and depleted, onto a drifting
iceberg in the warming arctic. I wish he'd swum instead

to Seattle where surely he could have made a career
out of catching fish thrown over the heads of tourists

at The Public Market. I don't like leaving home any more
than that bear, so when I get off the phone, I waste time

searching online for wildlife on Whidbey Island, where
I plan to work on my fiction. I'm not worried about bears,

but learn that some visitors are "disturbed by owls."
When I was little, my father said The Owl would get me

if I misbehaved, but he always laughed to show me
it wasn't real. Here are the names of some owls from

Whidbey Island: Great Horned, Snowy, Barred, Barn.
When we are very young or old, we don't always know

what is true. Meanwhile, there's always fiction. I love
the sounds owls make in the darkness. One answered me

as I hooted into the woods from my own front porch.
So I wrote this poem. I swear I didn't make that up.

At the Women's Writing Retreat

A key ring with a rape whistle. A
hard hat on a hook because I was in
earthquake territory now, they told me.
An air horn next to the tightly-made bed:

double safe, they said. But my flashlight
barely poked a hole in the cold black fog
after dinner and the sleeping loft stairs
were a dare I took, aged nine. Except I'd

just turned sixty. In my cabin's journal,
someone's large hand swore no one could
write well there unless she also ran nightly
through the woods, naked. In smaller print,

somebody else's: *Owl attack! He swooped
and I felt claws on my scalp as we hiked
back uphill, late.* I loved it all. Exactly one
blue plate, one mug, one set of flatware in

the kitchen, red-yolked eggs I cooked only
for myself. Dribbles of Northwestern sun,
the ground spongy with pine needles: fear
and joy, a balance women have always parsed

like weather. The great storm gathering
three thousand miles away was hyperbole,
I decided. The ferry back to the mainland
was smooth as silence, the sky silver as fish.

Calling My Husband From Seattle During Hurricane Sandy

You can't believe you still have lights, that
there's been so little rain. My eyes burn, tired
of TV, phones, computers. *John and Chris*

won't leave Atlantic City, you say. *They're not
answering my calls.* No one's heard from
Terese, either, in Greenwich Village. *Eighty*

mile an hour gusts on our side of the storm,
I say, even though it's not my storm, not really.
Three thousand miles away, I have no claim to

anything but green and yellow flames of radar
engulfing my home coastline, the TV loop of
surf cursing boarded-up buildings, smashing

the same black beach again and again. *The eye
isn't here yet*, says someone with a microphone.
It's like hearing a bad diagnosis: my cold fingers,

how I yank on the quilt on my sister's guest bed
and shake. *Wind's picking up*, you say; *you'd
really hate this! Listen!* You sit in the rocker on

our front porch, pushing a phone into the gale.
Go in! I say. *I need to see what happens,* you say.
The next morning you admit a whole row of trees

fell at once, across the street: a whoosh, a clatter
of wind-blasted wood on wood that drove you
running to the basement. Now the generator's

purring, our cats and house safe. My parents
never lost power. No word from anyone else.
Nyack Beach is gone. Piermont's under water.

The cable's out. *Boxed mac and cheese is awful;
you were right*, you say. *And the leaves! All gone!
All of them! Every single leaf from every tree.*

That Was When

for Treavor

Four of us sat like a family outside
around the table with its green cloth,
beside a silent green creek, the trees

heavy and green, their crowns round as
bellies or breasts, our dinner warming
inside, the oven ticking to temperature,

the church across the creek empty, late
sun in its yellow windows. All of us gone
from the hard white light of the office.

Chimney swifts swooped above us. And
then came the harmless snarl of a little jet
bound for Newark—in between worlds,

in between words. That was when you
looked down into the sad mirror of your
cell phone and said *No. No, get out of*

town! to nobody. Soon we'd all know
what loss, what invisible, flightless
wings were already folding around us.

My Father's Smile

was the house quickly tidied for a party, a holiday,
piles of newspapers hidden in a bathtub behind the
shower curtain. It was the kind face he wore when my
sister and I were small and sang at dinner, a grinning

papier mache pumpkin he gave us to hold in a picture he
took for the cover of his company magazine, both of us
in braids and getting along for once. But his rage was
a trail of dirty coffee cups, paper clips, a jangle of coins

from his pockets: small change left after long days.
Real, but nothing worth holding back or banking. He'd
worked a bad job for all that anger. I wanted his smile
instead, the one that worked on my mother, the golden

whiskey-warmth of his approval, the wit he fizzed
at my friends who laughed in a ring around him, well
into his 90's. Except even then he made me furious. He
loved me that much. Why would he clean up for me?

Take A Number

My sister said he didn't know he was dying. I knew it,
and couldn't believe my knowing. I made up her bed and

she flew all night back East. I propped my cell phone on
top of our house phone, next to my pillow. Sleeplessness

stops both time and hope, but then I lost track of everything
and woke in the stubborn light of day. My father had refused

to fix his air conditioning, refused to replace his roof, refused
the hospital. So I drove to his house. *They're bringing in*

a glass bowl, he said to me; *Take a number.* I wanted that
to mean more than neurons gone rogue with lack of oxygen,

and asked if it were a lottery. *Yes,* he said. My brother arrived
with a story he'd written. The aide changed my father's shirt.

My brother put his journal down on the dresser. My father's
breathing seemed deeper. My brother and I talked about trains—

passenger and freight—and kept the cable news on his TV as
my father had ordered us to. We did not notice when he died.

Except then my sister was back in the room, and my father
was gone. I'd been alone, without brother or sister, when it

began, when my father had called it a cold, a nothing. I'd said
Your doctor's afraid you have pneumonia. And at the wake,

his doctor's wife took my arm and said, *Pneumonia, the old
man's friend.* It wasn't my father's friend. My father fought

his friends, his children, his wife. We were always shouting, always stomping out of rooms behind slammed-shut doors.

Whatever floated him past that couldn't be his friend, unless light really is that stubborn. Unless light has tides of its own.

In Parting

My sister said goodbye to my father
right after he died. She said goodbye,

that he'd been a good father, told me
he could maybe still hear her, hear

her on his way to be gone. By then
I was shivering. How long had I worn

my father's love like a wet overcoat
I could not bear to take off? It had

no warmth, just weight. I couldn't
say *Goodbye, good father*. I couldn't

escape from myself any more than
he could—until he did. He really did.

He was gone. The next night, the air
outside my parents' house was humid

and beautiful, full of songs and car horns:
the wide world going about its business.

Four Days Later

when my mother's aide and my sister
had tidied his room and left the useless
brown pill bottles on the table by his bed,

I stood in midday sun before his mirror,
and did not see myself or my father, only
light pouring onto white wallpaper, light

on bleached-clean sheets and pillows. We'd
buried him, sung "Solidarity Forever" at
his wake, snuck Irish whiskey in flimsy

paper cups from the water cooler. *He'd
have loved that*, said my brother, and
that was true. Except my father wasn't

there. The only thing left was light. That
morning, I'd awakened dreaming of him
in a bathrobe he'd worn in the 1950's.

He'd said hello, held up one hand and
smiled, his awful love for me an old key
he no longer needed. Its lock was gone.

Stepping Out of Sorrow

Maybe you can't. Maybe you have to
wait until sorrow steps out of you like
a ghost in an evening gown rising
from the victim of a movie car crash.

See how it's translucent, how it drinks
a champagne cocktail and charms
everyone? Sorrow has a little dog.
It's much less gloomy than anyone

expected. It has a whirlwind romance
with your old boyfriend's failed novel.
It's in black and white and makes your
parents feel young again. It's best

watched late at night, when you can't
sleep. It's a tradition at Christmastime.
So what if you're still spilled between
the sporty convertible and the tree,

observing the full moon, the wispy
night clouds fluttering by like white
curtains in a nursery? You're the one
not in on the joke. The one left behind.

One Last Fire

Why is it almost reassuring, this thick, grey shrug
of sky, my hands scrambling in my pockets for
gloves? We drove to Orchard Beach, where the

rain we hadn't noticed before needled us until we
turned back to the car. But I thought *One last
fire tonight.* Everything's brown as the deer who

are not even slightly afraid of us, brown as their
shaggy, winter-thick fur. It's cold. We know
cold. It's nothing you have to think about. It's

like having another spoonful of soup without
slowing down to taste it. Finish the bowl, find
a match. The moon's lost in clouds. One last fire.

Fair Enough

On the phone my sister says of course parents
don't love their children equally. I agree; it's
a Hollywood concept, like closure, which
does not exist, especially after a death. *Now,*

a mother with a challenge like you, she says,
a very intelligent child, clearly, but still...
My sister is always kind, I think, and watch
at least two dozen grackles descend on seed

I'd meant for goldfinches, not them, easily
landing on perches designed to collapse under
their weight, a flapping, funereal celebration of
black feathers and open beaks. *Always hungry,*

I think, and try to turn something that aches
into a shrug. I don't even know what it is or
if it's allowed to be real. The grackles fly off as
my husband comes outside. *Look,* he says, and

there are the two house finches, purple-headed,
his favorites. They are ravenous, also. *Those were
house pets in the 30's,* he says, *and they escaped.
See how well they've adapted to life in the wild?*

This Almost-Noon

The boxwood's new growth, molten green in
the sharp light of eleven o'clock reminds me that
our dead are all around us, silent and disguised
by a lava-rage of baby leaves this almost-noon.

It is easier to know this now than on winter days
when the whole world is its own ghost—even dawn
and sunset, which in February often require faith
to be perceived. Our dead are here, although I can't

say how. I also think they are not sad. When
the grey shade of one large cloud arrives and
then passes, the day nods and folds its hands, but
it is far from being gone. Someone is watching me

tell you this, someone is watching you read it. Water
in a blue glass, a blessing, sun on a white stucco wall.

Two Small Elephants

After a chain of dreams in which I was
neither student nor teacher but always
late and unprepared, this: my sister and
her husband appeared before me with

two small elephants, twig-grey and
friendly as dogs, their heads hip-high
as I bent to pet them. I could feel
muscles twitching the kites of their

ears and their skin was warm and soft
like my own, which was how I knew
they were real as the reeking, poorly-lit
elephant house at the Bronx Zoo in the

1960's, from which they did not come.
Nor were they political mascots, nor toys.
Brown dust was on their heads, dry mud
crumbling onto my fingers as I woke to

blue, sweeping shadows—a street lamp, a
cedar branch. Knowing then everything
I couldn't do was long ago completed,
I listened to the wind, and could sleep.

My Mother's 92nd Birthday, at the Restaurant
on the Hudson

She'd been saying she was really 93 for two years, since
my father died at that age. But Mom was only 90 then;
we'd just celebrated her birthday a few months before.
My father had sat in his electric wheelchair at her party,

waving a martini big as both my cupped hands. His drink
was clear as the glass that held it, an olive bobbing next
to his thumb. He'd looked almost young in his wool jacket
from Ireland, his long hair silver-white and slicked back

with water. He'd been enraged with me an hour before:
he'd have to enter the party with his aide instead of my
mother because of his wheelchair, his van, my small car.
My sister's friend, who'd come to play Bach flawlessly

on cello, needed to get back to the City. We'd needed
to stop arguing and arrive on time. The perfect room
we'd rented had Hudson views that felt like riding inside
a bubble. But my father shouted at me until I cried, so

I look eyeless in every picture. *He was okay once he
drank that great, big martini,* said one sister-in-law, and
she was right. But it was my mother's birthday, not his.
Or mine. Today, on the way to the riverside restaurant,

Mom says, *Sometimes I fall asleep and when I wake up,
I think your father is still there, in his chair.* She doesn't
look sad; she's just noting it. *I have dreams about him,*
I say. A tugboat nudges a red barge through whitecaps

towards Manhattan. Hudson tides ebb and flood twice
a day, run salt to clear, up river and down, Lake Tear
of the Clouds to The Battery. The restaurant's greeter
opens the door to my mother. *93?* he says. *Impossible!*

There Was A Time

For Ken

maybe two or three days after 9/11, when
forgetting all of history and the world outside

my own experience, I said to you, *I don't
know how we'll ever be happy again.* You

nodded and said nothing and I said *I mean
we'll be happy, but not the way we were*

before. You nodded a second time. No one
we loved had died in the attacks, but we

had smelled smoke from Manhattan, and
watched the quiet, warm sky each night. So

little had touched me before then it was like
the world never had wind. Now, both of us

are without fathers, you without a sister, too.
We lift the awkwardly-wrapped packages

of our days. They are astonishingly light and
sometimes we are giddy because of it. *Look,*

you say. There, as we drive past the reservoir,
above the empty-fingered trees, is the heron

who swallows wriggling carp from our creek,
waving the great blue benediction of her wings.

Washing Windows

I don't miss the task and I do: blue,
ammonia-reeking fluid, knuckles
banging wooden frames, grey leaks
caught in a bleach-ruined bath towel,

relative clarity. Now we hire someone;
then it was our job—or really mine, you
busy elsewhere, me buffing glass until
the sky went salmon and you came inside

to say, *You're brave to do that with the
sun down,* meaning we'd both see what
I'd missed in the morning. I didn't care.
I just wanted an end to it. Now there are

ladders, buckets, a white truck, strangers,
and a new, surgical exactitude of light
in the living room, as you fill the letters
into a crossword puzzle and our cats hide.

Unseasonable

The poinsettias need watering again today, April fifth,
and still bloom a red that seems lost, this confectionary
season. *It foreshadows Christ's blood on the Cross*, said

the man who donated dozens of them to the church
the week after Thanksgiving. He'd bought one in white
to symbolize Virgin Birth, but someone else grabbed it

at Epiphany. The last eight came home with us. They
would not die at St. Valentine's, or St. Patrick's. Or stop
blooming on Good Friday. At least that made sense—

sort of. I mixed them with my other house plants, which
are nowhere near as healthy, in hope it wouldn't look
like Christmas. It does anyway. My orchids drop their

pink and white, modernist blooms to spend years lolling
fat green tongues at me like the spoiled brats I suspect
they always have been. My wintered-over geraniums,

also blood red, refuse to bloom indoors. I hover over
the poinsettias, finger their soil for damp the way I'd
check the temperature of a child's bathwater. *We had*

to take them, I tell my husband. *Natalie said the church*
would throw them away. He nods. *Our Christmas Cactus*
blooms on Halloween, he says. I have no children. I don't

know who I am protecting, or what, or why I seem to be
so good at it. It's like they are outlaws and I'm hiding them
from the Cops of Spring, who pound on the door with

a warrant. Maybe that's why it's so windy, why the sun is so strong. *Go away*, I shout, *No one's here*. The poinsettias bloom on and on. I hurry upstairs to fill the watering can.

Menaced by Two Godzillas, Our White Orchid Blooms a Giant Bloom

The forecast is always snow. We'd begun to
accept that, but the day we noticed the bloom,

the outside world was an unmade bed in the
sort of hotel room that would make you lonely.

Which is not to say shabby, just a place you'd
recall, not miss. Inside, the orchid had sprung

a crazy wand—crooked, burdened by enormous
flowers white as the sky, or the trees or ground,

almost too white. Winter has been with us for
three months, and we are twenty years married.

Our orchids are the ghosts of arguments, brought
home the next day, praised by us both for their

blossoms' longevity. They are practical apologies,
until they turn into squat green spinsters and

never bud again. Except for this one, menaced by
two toy Godzillas I bought almost thirty years ago,

on a doomed honeymoon, trying to laugh off
what I knew I couldn't salvage. The green, toothy

monsters are what I kept when I left. I still pose
them, lizardy arms mauling empty air, feet frozen

in the act of stomping a miniature nothing next to
our orchid, which is in absurd bloom despite it all

and neither Valentine nor peace treaty. Of course,
it starts to snow again. Upstairs, our fat old cat

thumps off your lap onto the floor and you flap
the newspaper open with a sound like a bird rising.

Weddings, Funerals

Give me a good funeral any day, says my husband
as he sets down a briefcase full of sheet music and his
organ shoes in the kitchen. He picks up our black cat
to explain himself. *There's no mother of the bride!*

He doesn't really mean it. The cat wriggles through
his tired fingers. O, endless eulogies! O, groomsmen
arriving drunk! O, light yellowed by church windows
and me trying not to weep over one woman's 104 years

or another's 56. My husband plays "The Bridal Chorus"
from *Lohengrin.* Even that makes me cry; *I'd never
have chosen it, I think,* and then wish I had. Assisting
in the choir loft, I lean to his ear with news: *The casket*

*has arrived from the funeral home. The priest is
still stuck in traffic. The bride is still not here. The
sister-in-law of the deceased has decided to sing
"Ave Maria." She says she doesn't have music.*

Someone's step taps the stairs. I blink tears from
my eyelashes, pretending to search for a tin of mints
in my purse. My husband flattens *One Hundred
and One Favorites* on the music rack, and looks up.

Teaching My Goddaughter About Turkey Buzzards

for Juliet

She's already in college, her hair long as a winter night:
brown-black, thick, half of it striped eight different colors
and twisted into a bun behind her head like the memory
of an impossible dawn. She stands on rocky ground

in front of the house her parents have just bought and
scans the sky for surprises. *That's got to be a hawk,*
she says. Because there's little else I can still teach her,
I shake my head. *Nah. Turkey buzzard*, I say. She laughs,

used to that kind of disappointment. *See its wings.*
Curved. Like scythes! I tell her, proud of an easy simile
that happens to be wrong. Turkey buzzards take nothing
still breathing in the August sun. They are careful bankers

of what's already gone, balancing a homely budget, bulky
and awkward as they crash through the trees to roost. They
are sorrow that recycles itself not into joy but dailiness:
after a night of bad dreams, windows glowing early blue.

After the Ghost Investigation

The local writer on the paranormal with her camera,
electromagnetic meter, and infared thermometer, having
stayed, as she explained she must, long past sunset,

came back downstairs egg white-wan, silent. Her colleague,
with his day job in law enforcement, looked lost as the ring
of brown feathers left after a cat runs into the bushes.

You have them. We found you two. In the room beside our
bedroom, in the room behind my office. Her voice might
have been shaking. *Just old spirits who don't care to leave.*

Not harmful. The one upstairs doesn't know he's dead.
I offered brandy, which no one wanted. Later, alone, or
perhaps not, my husband and I went to bed and addressed

our new-found guests: *How are you, Mr. Ghost? No—that's
disrespectful! No—you can't really believe...* I turned off
our bedside lamp and the darkness I'd once understood

occupied itself fully, grew larger and larger—a black
bloodstain, a backwards mirror glinting what sorrow?
A distant headlight? Or just the flickerings ghosts know,

caught here if they *are* here, never driving away. *These
walls, see how they've changed from what they used to be?
Our bodies, too: how they change without our permission...*

...and see how long, how very long night lasts?

79

To the Ghosts in My House

We've made it to your season again—not
All Saint's, just plain old winter, sunlight
filtered by no leaf or blossom on walls white

as forever. The kitchen radiator finally on,
the smell of its new heat. And wind's distant
engine turning over, off behind the neighbor's

houses. This bright cold is why you stay in here,
I'm sure. And why I'd never turn you out—never
wave sage smoke that would probably set off

the fire alarm, never call my friend's Albanian
Orthodox priest, who specializes in exorcism.
Supposed it worked? I'd have dealt myself only

a losing hand of cold, too-short days. Without
ghosts, a house is a bad hotel, rank with fresh
paint, noisy with the cheap fads of the living.

Poem on a Line from Akhmatova

I shall eat blue grapes with those who are dead.
—Anna Akhmatova

After tonight's supper, when you had left the room,
a maybe-shadow crossed the kitchen with no one
attached to it. Across the creek, before we'd even

moved in, a white-haired man leaned on his cane
to watch our painters, then stepped onto an old,
grown-over road. And vanished in its brush and

broken asphalt. In Deerfield, Massachusetts, you
and I read of the 1704 massacre, then walked
through dripping June heat and dim, thin-walled

rooms with windowpanes small as my palm.
Those houses were still sad, black front doors
set in frames scrolled like gravestones. Please,

listen. No place is really empty. Take this fruit
in your hands and offer it. There is something more
than just remembering. Even if it's my great-aunt,

tan in her green and white summer shirtwaist.
She's on the phone, as always, standing behind
the back door's dented screen, one foot balanced

on a cold radiator, her leg hoisted waist-high. And I
am five. I want to go outside and have to crawl
beneath her. I see she also wears Hush Puppies,

nylons with seams, and a washed-out garter belt.
But she doesn't notice me. She twirls one finger
in her hair. Can't you hear what it is she's saying?

Hair (mine)

In my teens, it wasn't quite long enough to
sit on. But long enough to be long, hanging
down straight as a dropped rock, red-blonde
and usually right in front of my eyes. People

asked what I was hiding from, but it was the
opposite of hiding, that hair. It wasn't like my
guitar-callused fingertips (hip but unlovely).
Or like my thighs, my poor shamed thighs,

lost under maxi-skirts. It was my only A plus
outside of English class, a backlit waterfall
that glowed in in dim rooms. It made you look.
Even bowed under all that hair, I could feel

you look. I said I wanted all that to stop, but
I didn't really. I cut my hair in my thirties
because I thought I had to, but then permed
it out so wildly it could set things on fire. I

wouldn't show my breasts or my still-sorry
legs, but I blew my ringlets dry with my head
hung below my knees and mis-matched my
earrings. The man I stayed married to said

it took years before he could finally see my
face. I was old five minutes after that. Who
knew I'd like the quiet? Who knew I'd grow
tired of it? Now I have lamb's fleece, shiny

as noontime traffic. You'll look or you won't.
It's too silly, too important. I shake my head,
searching for the right words, and see mostly
my hair, how it frames just about everything.

House and Garden

The woman always wants an extra room,
for guests, he says, watching the buy-a-
house show on TV. That drops a sharp pebble
down the back of your boot. He continues:

The woman always thinks family will visit.
They should stay in a hotel. You think:
They're not even our family. You're kicking
them out anyway? You say sometimes

the woman wants a tiny house with a pup-
tent-sized sleeping loft. He hates the show
about tiny houses. He says tiny houses
are even harder to keep clean than normal-

sized ones and probably a Republican plot
to get us to accept less. You know that he
has never lived in a tiny house. You know
that he's certainly no expert on cleaning.

You think: maybe that woman who wants
the extra room really needs somewhere
to get away from her husband. You think
about your own mother, how much she

adored a good fight. And then you wonder
why Republicans would plot about thumb-
sized cottages painted in primary colors
with good kitchen design. After he's gone

to sleep, you wait for night to settle into you.
Even though it's cold, you're content sitting
outside in a porch rocker without a coat,
each breath turning to smoke in the darkness.

Sunset, far from the City

The sun behind a tall stone wall of clouds in the West
grew more and more luminous: pink and orange that
shouldn't even exist. My neighbor Art leaned on his
upside-down rake as he called out to me. He pointed

at the sky. So we talked, turned to it, not each other.
As the fire faded until I could barely see him, we
joked about groundhogs and one new-antlered deer
who eats everything he doesn't trample. Then I said

You'll have no light left to rake, and Art crossed back
into his own yard to somehow gather a pile of gold
maple leaves that seemed shattered bits of sun, left
to smolder in the dusk. He melted into a shadow

behind his house but still I heard his rake scratch.
And decided watching sunsets is like watching the sea.
Is watching fire set in anger like that, too? By then
it was silent, and the air was cold. And so I went in.

A Nice Lady

Is trust the trade-off, then, for not being
noted in the street? There is, of course,
the freedom to proceed without the heat

of men's eyes, to settle with coffee and
a book quietly, in public, and actually be
allowed to read: a nice lady. My past's

curtained by my hips, the knobs of my
knuckles, the sweet, grandmotherly
softness under my chin. Long-married,

church-going, worried mostly about
my aged mother and the goddamned
housework, I sit beside my husband

and watch thread-thin, crinkle-eyed
actresses on late-night talk shows toss
their dried rose petals into everyone's

dreams. They still look stunning! See?
The host behind his long desk actually
listens to what they say: a new movie

or at least a racy memoir. Experience is
sexy, age not so much. Trust me on this—
at least as much as you'd trust anyone

unheard, able to see and yet be unseen.
I move freely among you now. And I take
notes. It doesn't matter what I seem.

Tragedy Undone

I gave the assignment most years: how do you
make this end well? Do it in one scene, write it,
perform it for the class with your study group,

with simple costumes, on Friday. So, the Nurse
smuggles Juliet to Mantua, Macbeth tells his
wife to pipe down, Hamlet gets over himself,

Hester says *Screw the Letter and the horse all
of you rode in on.* Meanwhile, Dimmesdale
grows a pair. Daisy realizes that Gatsby and her

husband Tom are both trouble and walks out of
the too-hot hotel room to cool off at the movies.
Three skinny high school boys wrapped in

someone's cut-up red and green plaid Christmas
tablecloth, someone in his uncle's snazzy white
suit with big lapels, a red construction paper

A saucering the air like a frisbee. And laughter,
laughter. I never asked them *What was the
thing you just lost?* I didn't want them to see it

that way, to get used to bleak relief that comes
after two hours of for-real tears, to expect sorrow
to roll around like a curriculum: Hester in the

autumn, Gatsby right after the daffodils finish.
That's for the teachers. We don't know for a fact
if Shakespeare's birthday was also the date of

his death fifty-two years later. What I'm saying
is nothing is written in stone–not really. *I loved
all of your scenes. Happy weekend! You all aced it.*

Reading "Birches" Aloud in Robert Frost's Cabin

This happened years ago, before local kids
bought beer, broke in, trashed his main house.
His writing cabin was laid out as he'd left it:
cast iron fry pan on the stove, perhaps having

dried over a low flame after breakfast eggs.
It was just past dawn and though he'd died
forty years before, I smelled toast and butter.
His razor lay on the sink, on its side. The guide

from Middlebury asked us—all teachers of
high school English—who was working on
Frost that week. *I am*, I said, proud of being
just where I was. *Sit down*, she said, pointing

to a chair that faced straight into his fireplace.
Its springs poked me through the upholstery.
Read the one you're teaching now, she said,
handing me an old copy of *Collected Poems*.

The room was cold. *Birches*, I began, and
read it slowly, thinking all the time how I'd
told my students to be careful, to note the boy
alone in the woods with no peers, and how

an ice storm has crashed the crystal spheres.
How a twig—Nature itself—could lash an
open eye to tears. *A poem can be a beautiful
lie*, I'd warned. How could he say *Earth's*

the right place for love? I'd begged them not
to be fooled: he'd never believed that. I heard
my voice shake a little, the way breath strains
if you pick up a load that is almost too great.

The guide smiled when I finished, and I felt
unwelcome where I sat. He was there, still,
somehow hearing my thought. He wanted
my frizz of blonde hair and Navajo turquoise

out of his brown Vermont cottage. And then
his home was ruined and restored by kids who
couldn't quite get lost in his woods. That he'd
have expected. The ruin—not the restoration.

To Robert Bly

My undergraduate writing professor, who could pop
his cold blue eyes out of focus as if he were watching
the ancient stardust storm that made us all, intoned
your Vietnam War poems like liturgy. Snow, bones,

Minnesota: poems like the yearly cries of geese leaving.
But all I wanted was a boyfriend and an English muffin
in the Student Union, a place comforted by golden
stained-glass windows and the eternal sweetness

of frying onions. Years later, I brought my husband
to your reading because once, after tribal drumming
in a Truth or Consequences, New Mexico sweat lodge
with a group of men who freely quoted your writing,

he'd almost joined their swim across The Rio Grande.
You wore a red silk jacket, and spoke of many fathers.
You said the best poetry had at its heart SORROW, and
crossed the air before you with a fiery gesture: a song

itself. Know that my husband is a poor swimmer, a man
who seldom acts upon impulse, a man who seldom
reads poetry. Know that he sat rapt, red-faced, weeping,
not wiping his eyes. Afterwards, when we both shook

your hand, the scent of your sweat was pungent and
dense as all the world's SORROW: a laugh for the ride
home, a mean joke. But Robert—if I may call you that—
the Great Blue Heron who glides down our creek when

I am sad, a single fish glistening in her beak, speaks
to me of dark worlds beyond, of tears on the moon,
and God's breath in the night. She walks on stilt-legs,
then spreads her wings wide. She says you are right.

94

On *A Thanksgiving Anthem,* by William Billings

Ye dragons, whose contagious breath
People the corridors of death
Change your dire hissings into heavenly song
And praise your maker with your forked tongues.
—William Billings, 1794
(a paraphrase of Psalm 148)

For-ked, with two syllables, and at least five
sixteenth notes on "for". Repeatedly. For
measure after measure. *Breath control,*
says my husband. He reminds me it was

my idea our choir sing this anthem. It's what
I deserve for having cocktails with him and
a Sacred Harp CD. William Billings, leather
tanner, street sweeper, composer, missing

an eye, one leg shorter than the other, loved
dragons. Hissing dragons, especially, because
he could win even them. So what if they
smelled bad and King James gives them just

one word in Psalm 148? Billings turned his
anthem into dragons, turned his whole choir
into dragons, turned choirs into dragons two
hundred and twenty years into the future.

And because of his love, the dragons were
grateful. They unfolded their napkins and
ate turkey and Indian Pudding. *Make sure*
you hit the "s" in "hissings", my husband says:

Hissssingss! Thus instructed, our lizard-like
scales include the whole world, as they were
intended to. See? The dragons are carrying
everyone's plates to the kitchen sink. *Alleluia!*

Twenty Years

I turn over a halved winter tomato
in the fry pan and it looks like the decent
B&B our first time in England, my belly
poking against the waistband of my jeans,

our last-night's landlady presenting us
with scones we're too full to eat, and then
must. The backpack you insisted I buy
leans against the wall near the door

for the hike back downhill to the train.
Your hair is grey already, but I still worry
about being pregnant. I'm not. There are
no cell phones yet. Europe means a cheap

flight on a prop plane across The North Sea
delayed by someone faking a heart attack
on the runway, after seeing the cabin. (Not me.)
Two calls home all summer. My father saying

This is London as I hold the receiver out
of the booth so he can hear Big Ben strike six.
You and I sure we don't want kids. My parents
fine as they'd ever been, fine in small doses,

not needing us; my mother still reading
books I buy for her. Now we pack suitcases;
we fill entire trunks of cars. And the tomato
is sweet-sour, soft from cooking; red-brown

juice and seeds run into our scrambled eggs.
Now when the phone rings, we both stop
talking. *Yes,* you say to someone. You hold
a hand up. *Nothing,* you mouth. *It's nothing.*

On Hearing an Old Recording of Your Voice

for Ken, after twenty years

It's not like you in old photos, except for being
very present but almost impossibly thin, and

you were surely both at twenty-three. There's no
familiar undertone, no clue you still own, just

a tenor agile and slight as the hooked neck
of a swan. Haydn, a mass. A custom recording,

Riverside Church, NYC. *I have no memory of
singing this*, you say, and slip the LP back in its

white jacket. But you're listed with the others:
soloist. Long before I knew you. And now there

are days I've lost, too: little towns in Germany
dropped from the snapped necklace of what I

recall, all the rooms I woke in warm darkness
beside you with no idea where I was. Drunks

shouted in my grandmother's language outside
our open windows. I couldn't understand, only

trust we'd find our way to Berlin and then home.
I stand still amazed that we didn't lose each other

entirely in the haze of what happened long ago,
me thinner too, but far less patient, and you—your

laugh already huge—growing sunward in some
blessed direction neither one of us could know.

Younglings

Younglings squint in the early spring
sunshine outside their first apartments,
hair wet, beds made, pajamas dumped

in the wash, something half-ruined worn
to the laundromat. The boyfriend with the
old soul won't clean the cat's box or rinse

the bathtub. And there's work in the morning!
Sorrow, damp mossy sorrow rises like the
scent of their mother's basements—and at

odd times: crossing midtown streets, after
dinner on a Sunday night, watching the
tail lights of cars heading back upstate.

Someone else is laughing with a table full
of friends. Someone else got the job they
interviewed for twice. The year's a third

spent and the rest of its months won't take
forever anymore. Which is fine if you don't
remember what you really hoped for or even

if you hope for it still. *Listen,* I want to say.
*It's easier to be old, to have already gotten
divorced, lost your lease, easier to have had*

the operation with general anesthesia. You'll
have survived by the time you're old. Now, the
frantic joy of breathing at seventeen is gone

like the weekend, and nothing, nothing can
replace it. Except that something will. Listen
to the stars buzzing above you. Listen harder.

Driving by My Old Houses at Night

They're lanterns of someone else's life now.
Baby-proof screening's on the upstairs porch
where my husband and I, wrapped in quilts,

could almost see the New Year's fireworks,
and never had kids. Did we ever watch
so much TV? The living room's blue with it,

but the new owners have kept our curtains.
That old commune where I alone took down
Christmas trees and wiped formica counters—

is it still a rental? TV's on there, too, always.
My prettiest place—barroom and kitchen
of an old resort hotel turned to apartments—

is never lit. I washed those dark windows,
cooked veal chops there for a man who never
loved me, and survived not being loved. It was

easier than you'd think, easier than I thought,
but hard to explain as empty air holding a bird
in flight. Momentum, velocity—maybe time.

Dr. Haller Nutt's Half-Built, Octagonal Mansion

Longwood Plantation, Natchez, Mississippi

For one hundred years, his family lived on in its cellar,
the upstairs walls sketched in raw lumber on bare brick.
Construction steps still spiral their dizzy geometry

five stories up inside the dome. But by 1861, he'd frilled
each porch column in wooden lace. The huge roof and
Great War were on. Dr. Nutt owned 800 slaves, and died

before the end of hostilities. Left his daughters to play
with salesmen's models of never-delivered chairs. Left us
this unimaginable eight-sided loss: pneumonia, poverty,

a paralyzing void passed generation to generation. Left us
the smell of clay, dust swimming in sunlight, a bench lined
in rusty tools, a piano's empty shipping case tipped on its

side, grey as an cast-off bandage. You can buy a ticket, or
rent the place for your holiday party. Everyone knew this
could never be finished. Everyone knows it still isn't done.

Los Alamos, On The 50th Anniversary of The Trinity Test

July 16, 1995

Now we are all sons of bitches.
—Kenneth Bainbridge to J. Robert Oppenheimer

It was a Roadrunner cartoon until then: up
mesas and down, brown stone and sand, sky blue
and windless. We kept the car's air conditioner
cranked until our fingers ached, but sweat dried

on our arms the minute we walked into sunlight;
I could lick the back of my hand and taste salt.
I wore a leather cowboy hat from Australia with
my white sundress and sandals, and was afraid

to go into the museum. As if knowing it was there
heated the whole desert, as if I were still twelve,
awakened before dawn by sirens, praying to not
count ten three times: the civil defense code. As if

a red transistor radio were still under my pillow and
"Don't Let The Rain Come Down" my only proof
of nothing incoming: *Ah-ah, oh no.* You and I had
forgotten the big birthday, didn't know there'd be

scientists our parents' age on line with us, pointing
at mock-ups of their old living rooms, linking fingers
with their smiling wives. I didn't know how hard I'd
want to hate them, especially one man who laughed

at the Trinitite: a green blob of desert sand fused
in the explosion, a ruined church window. *Yeah, I
grabbed me some of that stuff! Wear it on a string
around my neck if I'm catching cold! Works great!*

But they were silent in the room with the black ghosts:
pictures from Hiroshima of men and women turned
to photographs themselves by the fire such good people
could make. I didn't hate anyone, then. I couldn't hate.

Hibakusha

In Japanese, Hibakusha means "bomb-affected people." It is the term used for survivors of the atomic attacks on Hiroshima and Nagasaki.

If we carry everything that ever happened to us, words
must be the buckets we use to contain it all. That was the

first thing I thought as I opened my eyes to day gathering
itself into one bird and then many, into harmless light

that grew until I got up to join familiar trees and a
road crew listening to talk radio out the open windows

of their truck. They were laughing as I opened our door
to pick up the newspaper in its blue plastic bag and I

thought how the Hibakusha I'd gone to hear last night
had laughed, too: at snotty noses they'd had the winter

after the A-bomb, at the translator interrupting their
Japanese with English too soon, or not soon enough.

I understand almost no Japanese, so it all sounded like
rain to me. I do understand rain. Then the grandmother—

her three-legged cane leaning on the lectern—cried.
It was her twelve-year-old best friend in 1945 again,

dying of radiation burns, said the translator, dead fish
suddenly floating in the river, how her mother said they

were poison and made her put them all back, the black
rain. At the end of the evening, someone bowed to me

and gave me a lapel pin with a pink flower that said 70
years, and a packet of shrimp crackers from Hiroshima.

Today, I have no words. How can we plan these things
in the light of morning? How can we mock the sun and

actually teach it as history? Someone said *Yes, go do this*.
Someone named the bomber after his mother. And then

someone else looked up into the blue sky, saw the glint
of an approaching plane and thought, *Oh! How pretty!*

Looking at Manhattan from the Tappan
Zee Bridge

It's fish-bone frail from up here, half-dissolved on the
horizon. The brown Hudson pulses with wind, and I
consider the usual portents of our destruction. Always,

the bullseye centers on Times Square. Firestorms or gas
or radiation orbits in tight and tighter rings of deepening
dread. Asteroids, terrorists, plagues: we direct them all

here to illustrate the legions dead, and who might survive.
On northbound trains in high school, I breathed slower
with each station behind me. But how to lose the cut crystal

of those streets at night, the electric glitter caught in sour
black puddles and dark office windows? How to forget
the seventeenth century silversmith with my father's name?

After 9/11, we drove to western Massachusetts, but I
couldn't sleep in the loneliness there. The whole world had
been lost somewhere outside those lovely little towns; some

great light was gone. Manhattan's mute at this distance,
but the sun it shares with me is ancient, Dutch, seafaring.
I hear my own heart beat in its silence: home, home, home.

This Dangerous Agreement

July 4, 1776–July 4, 2017

I've always wondered how they managed it,
in July, in Philadelphia, wearing wool and wigs
in a wooden building that sings in the wind,

still. I know that part because I heard it once,
the sound a cello note in horizontal rain driven
against its tall, many-paned windows. Except

the sun shone the day Jefferson observed, upon
awakening, sixty-eight degrees—not even eighty
that afternoon—and only a few clouds. They started

us then, after days of ink and revision, argument's
bark and buzz, lavender-scented hair powder,
footsteps and the scrape of chairs pushed back

in a loud, high-ceilinged room. They came
to this dangerous agreement. It was not perfect,
but it was beautiful. The right to seek joy freely

granted, and worth everything else: rocky hills
beyond green ones, rivers with silver and brown
currents and the sequined tangle of many cities

at their mouths. The daily celebration, the
shouting match. And this dangerous agreement.
The founders could have been hanged for it.

It was not perfect, but it lives in our breath
even when we're afraid it has been lost. We'll
find it again. We were born with that right,

the eighteenth century ticking its logic
in our heartbeat, in our laughter and hopeful
chatter after dinner as evening gathers.

Sorrow blows into joy with our seeking, like
cool air after thunder, like fireworks from the
next town over, blooming high above dark trees.

Spring Twilight

I'm always a child at this time of year,
watching the season advance through
two small windows at the sides of my
parents' fireplace, in our first house.

Here's the hearth's smooth grey stone—
river rocks I can cup my hands over—
under our thick, mahogany mantel. No
lamps shine, only the deep green end

of day: green like my grandmother's
glass coffee cups, like watercolors, or new
backyard moss. The trees have no leaves
but the grass is luminous and forsythia

that blazed yellow a week ago is now
smoldering green. My parents are quietly
elsewhere, my sister, my great aunt. Joy
has caught up with me for no good reason.

I've done nothing to deserve it. Even now.
None of us has done anything to deserve
joy. It's just present: all those gentle grey
clouds. That still, wet air. This sweet green.

My Mother Wants to Look at the River

Now she's down to three—or maybe four—
stories that make up her Book of Hours,
the psalm *A Night Out Before I Met Your*

Father, The Litany of Lost Pets. Drive her
to the Hudson and she'll say, *Look at that
beautiful river!* The first law of dementia

is that everyone has to agree with you, but
still, there's no possible argument. Look!
Illuminated, blue, green, grey, silver, tree-

fringed or bound with the rough jewelry of
the new Tappan Zee Bridge construction,
the River is more than I could tell you with

all my wits, all my poems. All my life, away
from home, I've always picked the window
near the water, but there is no other water,

really. The great sea pounds its chest over
and over outside your vacation cottage, or you
fly over the flash of its vastness, knowing

but for this one cheat of physics, it would
swallow you. But The Hudson says this:
Come, sit. Your grandfather drove across

*before there was a bridge, during a hard
freeze, on the ice. Did you know? There
were sloops, The Ghost Fleet, a long iron*

chain from West Point to Constitution
Island, during the Revolution. These were
*your people, living her*e. Maybe my mother

hears it. She smiles and says nothing. I watch
the tides countering each other, note the
track of the wind, the safety on the other side.

About the Author

Christine Potter has been a cook and a teacher of literature and creative writing. These days, she is a writer and poet who lives in the lower Hudson River Valley with her organist/choir director husband Ken, and two spoiled cats. Her house is very old, and has ghosts. Her two other collections of poetry are *Sheltering in Place* (2013, Cherry Grove Collections) and *Zero Degrees At First Light* (2006, David Robert Books). Christine's time-traveling young adult novels, *The Bean Books,* are published by Evernight Teen: *Time Runs Away With Her, In Her Own Time,* and *What Time Is It There?*

www.ingramcontent.com/pod-product-compliance
Lightning Source LLC
Chambersburg PA
CBHW051431090426
42737CB00014B/2915